THE PROBLEM THAT DESTROYS RELATIONSHIPS

THE PROBLEM THAT DESTROYS RELATIONSHIPS

GR8 RELATIONSHIPS

EQUIP PRESS

Colorado Springs

THE PROBLEM THAT DESTROYS RELATIONSHIPS

Published by Equip Press, Colorado Springs, CO

First Edition: 2022
The Problem That Destroys Relationships / (GR8 Relationships)
Paperback ISBN: : 978-1-958585-17-7
eBook ISBN: 978-1-958585-18-4

EQUIP PRESS

Colorado Springs

CONTENTS

INTRODUCTION

What is the problem that destroys relationships? God has given us a perfect design for relationships. He even fashioned men and women in roles that support that design. So why do so many marriages end up in shambles? Why is it that so many people who once planned their lives, hopes, and dreams together find themselves going in opposite directions?

It's simple.

Think about a baby. The innocent child is totally dependent on crying to get what he or she wants. A baby literally only knows that everything is about them.

The baby makes everything about *ME*.

"I'm hungry, you need to feed me, so I'm going to cry until you do."

"My diaper is wet; I'm going to cry until you change it."

"It's the middle of the night and I don't know where you are, so I'm going to holler until you pick me up and rock me to sleep."

Unfortunately, those sweet innocent babies become grown up babies!

When you are struggling in a relationship and looking for someone one to blame, don't you typically point your finger at the other person?

Do you find yourself thinking or saying these phrases?

"You need to do it my way."
"You need to make me happy."
"You need to change." (I am okay, you aren't!)

These phrases are indicators that your *ME* is flashing. Your *ME* is flashing? In case it is new for you, here's the concept.

The Flashing ME

You might be wondering what *Flashing ME* means. More than likely, it's your biggest problem, and exactly what it sounds like. Your *ME* is your focus. It demands that you serve yourself, demand your way and focus on yourself more than focusing on or serving others.

The fact that you may not see how often you focus on yourself, that is on *ME*, is a sad thought. When other people are selfish and self-absorbed, you notice, but not when you do it. Is that true for you? It is for me.

When others are selfish, it is like they have the word *ME* flashing on their forehead. But when I do it, I cannot see it, because it is on my forehead above my eyes. You can be totally selfish, not interested in serving others, which means your *ME* is flashing bright enough to light a house, but you do not see it. You can look at this another way and ask yourself if you are acting like a baby.

Are You Acting Like a Baby?

Think about that grown up baby I mentioned. Is that you? A baby is a good picture of how the problem works. Not the picture of a cuddly and innocent baby, but an out-of-control, screaming infant who wants something. That's another good name for the problem: The Baby.

Simply put, the Baby plugs into the sin nature, which is plugged into the world, which is ruled by Satan himself. As the Baby you take everything personally, which makes your *ME* flash.

Defensiveness is the primary reaction of the Baby, especially when you are criticized. You live primarily by appetites, impulses, and pleasures. You focus on selfishness, self-absorption, and self-sufficiency: "it's all about *ME*."

This problem is built-in and is part of everyone. Those without the life of Christ and the Spirit of God in them are slaves to that *ME* behavior.

Those of us who have trusted Jesus's death, burial, and resurrection as the answer for our sin have a choice, *the* fundamental choice: trust God or trust something or someone other than God. Present yourself to righteousness or unrighteousness, as it says in Romans.

> *And do not present your members as instruments of unrighteousness to sin but present yourselves to God as being alive from the dead, and your members as instruments of righteousness to God.*

Romans 6:13, NKJV

Most people act like The Baby.

You have built-in desires including being accepted, feeling included, significant, valuable, close, secure, safe, cared for, and satisfied. And when you fear you will not get those, and others like them, your *ME* starts flashing. So, admitting your tendency to be self-absorbed is not easy.

You will excuse your behavior with statements like "If I don't look out for myself, who will?" But you do not have to choose self-absorption. That mindset or behavior is the default of your sin nature, or a life that trusts something other than God. The chart below shows the human nature tendency to certain actions and mindsets based on our sin nature, which is self-focused rather than other-focused. The right side of the chart gives some solutions to deal with our natural tendencies.

Making Everything About Me

Make everything about me	
THINKING/ACTION	SOLUTION
Be defensive	Be teachable
Be self-absorbed	Be considerate
Be self-indulgent	Be self-controlled
Work on your self-esteem	Accept who you are
Be a victim	Make choices
Always be right	Seek truth
Seek revenge	Forgive
Be manipulative	Tell the truth
React and respond	Choose and create
Be unilateral, self-serving	Pursue others' best

Looking at the chart above, do you recognize any of your own behaviors? When first presented with the idea of the Flashing *ME*, you might bristle at the fact that you are self-absorbed, or even refute the notion that most people live in Flashing *ME* mode.

What is the fundamental element that destroys relationships? People thinking more about themselves than the needs of others. People not realizing that their ME is flashing at everyone, and since it is on their forehead, everyone can see it except them!

REFLECTIVE QUESTIONS

- What is your reaction to the idea of your Flashing ME?

_____

_____

_____

_____

- Describe a situation where you thought, "If I don't look out for myself, who will?" How did the situation play out? How could it have been different if you weren't focused on you?

_____

_____

_____

_____

- Describe a recent situation when you were angry, irritated, or upset with someone. Do you believe that you were _Flashing your ME_ then? If so, how could you have changed your perspective to _pursue their best_?

_____

_____

_____

_____

_____

- If you find yourself thinking or saying the
  phrases listed below, then your ME is flashing.
  Track how often you here yourself thinking
  these things or something similar over the next
  three weeks. Make a note of the situation and
  the relationship you have with the other person.
  "You need to do it my way."
  "You need to make me happy."
  "You need to change." (I am okay, you aren't!)

_____

_____

_____

_____

_____

- Notice when you are acting like the Baby. What
  prompted your behavior?

_____

_____

_____

_____

_____

THE FOUR BIG MISTAKES

The problem that destroys relationships displays itself in at least four big mistakes. We have given these mistakes names:

- The Politician
- The Victim
- The Actor
- The Dictator

The Politician

The Politician operates based on opinion and emotion. When they need an explanation for something, if they don't have all the facts, they will fill-in-the-blanks with conjecture rather than researching or understanding all the facts. The emotion the Politician adds to the facts often makes them seem more believable to others.

That is an unfortunate, yet consistent pattern in relationships – filling-in-the-blanks about what happened rather than looking for the facts. It is also, a pattern people have regarding God, speculating about what He is doing and worse, who He is.

The word *think* is used seventy-two times in the New King James Version of the Bible. Much of the time the word think is used as a synonym for opinion or speculation. Here are some examples,

> *Do you think this is right? Do you say, My*
> *righteousness is more than God's?*

Job 35:2, NKJV

> *Do not think that I came to bring peace on earth.*
> *I did not come to bring peace but a sword.*

Matthew 10:34, NKJV

God wants your thinking to align with truth because He wants to protect you from error. Too often, error arises from depending on opinions, speculations, or guesses instead of the facts.

Start to notice when you operate based on opinion, rather than the truth or facts. Consider a recent difficult conversation you had, especially one involving *elevated negative emotions* (ENE's). How much speculation and opinion were present? What did you claim about the other person that you did not know as a clear fact? What did they claim about you that was not fact? Did the claims and speculation help or hurt your relationship at that time?

The speculations, opinions and claims most often lead to further accusations and often actions based primarily on the speculation. A chain of events starts because of opinion, claims, and guesses rather than facts. And the worst part, you may have seen this also, further problems were created, or the problem was inflamed because of the speculation.

Opinion

The definition of opinion from Webster's Collegiate Dictionary is as follows:

> *Judgment or belief not founded on certainty or proof; the prevailing or popular feeling or view: public opinion; belief stronger than impression and less strong than positive knowledge.*
> *Synonyms—evaluation, estimation, conjecture, supposition, theory*

The definition reveals some important information. "Belief not founded on certainty or proof." Synonyms include: conjecture, supposition, and theory.

In order to aid relationships and clarify conversations, consider this option: you are in a conversation and about to state something that you do not or cannot know as a fact.

You stop yourself and say, "My speculation is . . ."

Better yet, what if you said, "I am only guessing here, so be careful with what I am offering. My guess is . . ."

The point is to let others know when you are filling-in-the-blanks. Having an opinion is valid. Everyone has one. Some have lots. Just be honest about what is fact and truth and what is your opinion. Remember, you have three options to categorize anything in your mind. Is it truth, a lie, or an opinion. When you assess your thought process, you may be surprised at how much of the time you adopt your opinion as fact, even if you don't verbalize it.

If something is true, it is not an opinion, because it is right, a fact. If something is false, it also is not an opinion, because it is wrong, a fact. For falsehoods, obviously, do not believe and stop using them. Unfortunately, many people are not willing to see a falsehood as a lie and just move it into the opinion or even truth category, because it just seems *right*. Finally, if it is an opinion, that means you do not know enough about it to determine whether it is true or false. Be diligent and search for the facts. And be careful if you use the *fact,* because it may be wrong.

Consider the following:

- Just because I believe something, that does not make it true. Truth is not impacted by your belief.

- Am I guessing about life and relationships, not seeking the truth or facts?
- Is my life based on opinions, maybe even lies that have not been verified?
- Do I know the "Who said so," the facts and truth that support my beliefs?
- My opinion may be false. Do I know the consequences?
- Simple probability says that my opinion has a 50 percent chance of being a lie.

Truth

Jesus is dedicated to helping you think clearly. But the lack of knowledge about who He is, the lack of being in His Word leaves you with nothing more than an opinion about Him. He wants you to depend on Him and His Word and stop depending on yourself (and other things) that do not provide an accurate understanding of who He is.

God's Word states this clearly,

Trust in the Lord with all your heart and lean not on your own understanding; in all your ways acknowledge Him and He will direct your paths.

Proverbs 3:5-6, NKJV

Truth is superior to opinion. Truth does not need to be defended, because it will stand when all else fails. Opinion believes and operates as if it knows everything. When you do that, you are depending on yourself instead of God.

Stop dancing around the truth and look at it. Check out the definitions of words and precisely define the problems and issues you are struggling with. Without truth you will not be wise; instead, you will be weak and vulnerable.

Facts or Opinion

Peter Scholtes performed some research about fact-versus-opinion in a manufacturing environment where empirical data is available. He wondered how convinced and assertive people would act if they only had an opinion about something. He discovered that people were absolutely convinced about what they were saying, but it was not correct, it was not true.

Scholtes concluded, "Without data, opinion prevails. Where opinion prevails, whoever has power is king. The ultimate correlation, therefore, is more likely between assertiveness and clout, not assertiveness and objective truth."[1] So if you are a leader or in a position of power, you may quickly ignore the facts and aggressively push your opinion because you have the power. The same thing happens in relationships, right?

You can believe something about another person, but the facts do not support what you believe. In fact, what you believe could be lies that you may be passing along to others. Talk about hurting relationships! Worse yet, that behavior implies you may be doing the same thing in other areas of your life.

You can determine how much you rely on opinion and assumptions by asking some simple questions:

Do you accept or believe something that has little or no evidence to support it?

Do you say things like "How can we know truth?"

Or you say or believe, "Truth is how you see it."

Of course, phrases like these mean you probably believe that there are no absolutes.

If so, you operate with opinion and assumption more than searching for objective data. If your foundation is opinion, then that can easily lead to confusion and sin because it trusts something other than God.

Specifically, you might believe that the Bible is more opinion rather than objective truth. If so, do some research (if you are willing to table your opinion for a time). When you study the facts you will see the Bible is trustworthy and accurate. While faith is still required, it is not needed to see the objective facts about the overwhelming textual, historical, and geographical validity and accuracy of the Bible.

Faith always plays a part in your life because that is the structure God created.

That means opinion is needed in the realm of "I do not know enough to know whether this is true or false."

It is impossible to live daily without making assumptions or having an opinion about something. But that is not the issue. It is whether you clearly decide to act or believe the opinion or assumption as if it is truth or a lie. That is the issue, your *belief in the opinion*. So, hold your opinions, speculations, assumptions, and guesses without grasping them tightly. And let others know this is just your *guess* or *speculation*.

More importantly, do you believe your opinion about God's Word rather than what God clearly states in His Word? That causes horrible problems for relationships, because the end result is you trust what you want to do rather than what God says.

While opinion and assumption are part of life, that does not mean God is hiding things you need to know. Consider what God tells us:

> . . . *as His divine power has given to us all things that pertain to life and godliness* . . .
>
> **2 Peter 1:3, NKJV**

What you need *has been given* to you!

When you operate with opinion, you don't know the facts because you are not in the Bible enough. Which further implies that you trust other sources, even yourself, more than God's Word. Only you and God know the objective reply to that statement.

So, to avoid the politician mode stick to the truth, the objective facts, not your opinions and emotions. The politician relies on himself or herself rather than God's truth.

Reflections—The Politician Scenario

Consider the scenario below and identify where the Politician is at play, espousing opinions rather than truth.

Ginger and Sam have been married ten years and have not been able to have children, so their two dogs and two cats are their kids. Both of them work at the local high school, so time in the evening is often spent on lesson plans and high school activities. Here's a conversation they had over dinner one night at the kitchen table in their modest three-bedroom home.

Ginger asked, "Sam, how was your day today?"

"Same as always."

"Anything new going on with that basketball team you are coaching?" she asked with a smile.

"No, none of them really want to work very hard," he said as he looked down at his food.

"Oh?" she queried.

"You know, you watch them in practice, and they don't follow the plays, even though they all played basketball in junior high. I know their coach taught them these basic plays. Every basketball team uses them. It's really frustrating to work with underachievers."

He stopped and looked up at her because he knew she was waiting to spill all the details of her day. He thought to himself, "I don't know why a woman as smart as her feels she needs to talk about every last detail of everything in her life."

"Well, we had some new students in Math class today. They are merging the two high schools into one special Math program. I'm really excited because these are really bright kids, and they want to go somewhere in life."

"Great," he answered trying to show excitement. "How do you know they are bright. Not all the kids from the other high school know everything."

"I checked their aptitude scores, and we do special testing to see if they fit in the program."

"How do you know they want to go somewhere in life?"

Ginger smiled brightly, "I admit, I don't know that for sure. My opinion is that many of them will move forward in life because of their natural and instinctive curiosity and learning new information and exploring concepts they haven't learned before."

REFLECTIVE QUESTIONS

- What did you notice in this scenario about what Sam and Ginger thought or said that relates to the Politician mistake?

_____

_____

_____

_____

- Think about your own life. Identify some situations where you have made the Politician mistake. How did that impact your relationships with others? What could you do differently the next time?

_____

_____

_____

_____

The Victim

Victims live in the past. Here's a list of what you do if you act like a victim:

- Keep a detailed log of everything bad anyone has ever done to you. Read the list daily and pick at least two items to bring up that day.

- Never live for today or hope for tomorrow. Only focus on how you have been mistreated in the past.
- If you tire of thinking how you have been mistreated, think of all the bad things you did to others, and believe that others will never forgive you, or if they did, they did not mean it.
- Consume every day with what happened in the past, with *how it was*. Never tire of bringing up the same issue repeatedly, *ad nauseam*.

The above list may seem extreme, but you probably have done some of that. I know I have. Acting like a victim requires focusing on the past as if it were today. The attitude of wanting to change the past keeps the past in the present. Of course, remembering the past is not always bad. You can use the past wisely by remembering how God has provided, protected, and blessed you. Here's what Hebrews says.

> *But recall the former days in which, after you were illuminated, you endured a great struggle with sufferings . . .*

Hebrews 10:32, NKJV

Too often, we remember only the bad things, which destroys you by turning you into a victim who must be rescued. Victims cannot be helped, only rescued. If you find yourself complaining a lot, you probably have become a victim. You have an option to change by taking responsibility for your choices and being thankful in all things.

Victims say, "If everyone else would get their act together, my life would be better."

The lack of personal responsibility creates a structure to blame others for life's circumstances. So that when everyone else around you makes the changes that you require, you will be rescued. The amount of time you stay in this mindset depends on how much you trust in a perfect God.

You can keep the past in the present in numerous ways based on whether others have wronged you, or you have wronged them. When others have wronged you, here are some consequences of thinking like a victim. You will:

- Hold grudges, store up resentments, and become bitter.
- Drag the problem into as many of your other relationships as possible.
- Enlist others to join the *cause* against the *jerk*.
- Let everyone know it is their job to help or rescue you.

When you wrong others, you will employ the following.

- Self-punishment or shame. For example, "I'll never be able to get over this."
- Scapegoating (blame) – "They are the problem. I wouldn't have done it if they…"
- Penance (good deeds) – "I'll make it up to them by . . . "
- Attempt self-forgiveness – "I know that others and even God has forgiven me, but I just can't forgive myself!"

These actions enslave rather than free you. But if you are playing the victim you cannot see that. You become a slave to the very circumstances, events, and people that you do not like or who hurt you.

Two critical tools can help you when the past controls you. Those tools include:

- Forgiveness – when others have harmed you
- Confession – when you have harmed others

Resolution

Taking the past out of the present means you deal effectively with conflict. A critical component of our

Conflict RESOLVED workshop is the fact that conflict is an opportunity for growth and development.

Basically, all conflicts have the potential to turn into destructive, endless cycles. Start at the top with Tension. Something happens between you and another person that creates tension. Role Dilemma is next, or the *blame game*, where each of you are saying, "It's your fault, not mine."

That leads to Gathering Injustices, building the case that it was their fault, not yours. Once there is enough evidence, you or they are ready for a Confrontation. The confrontation leads to Adjusting, which can have numerous options. Here are four of that are common:

First, the evidence used was not effective, so you or the other person decide to throw fuel on the fire by bringing up other **unresolved conflicts**.

A second option is like the end of a round in a **boxing match**. Each of you "go to your corners" to gather more evidence to prove that the problem is because of the other person.

A third option happens when either person says, "I'm out of here." They **run away from conflict**, which often looks like resolution, but the conflict has not been resolved, it is just out of sight or dormant. This option places another obstacle between you and the other person that will stay there, keeping the two of you apart until this conflict is resolved.

The fourth option, **Resolution**, ends the cycle. When conflict is seen as a possibility for growth and development, resolution is more likely. Without resolution, the conflict cycle will help keep the past alive, separating the two of you and reducing the quality of your relationship.

Dr. Fred Lybrand has a great quote that is worth memorizing:

> *"Good marriages and relationships leave a trail of resolved issues."*

That puts the right picture in your mind. Consider two people walking side by side on a path or on the beach. They are like the picture here, close enough to be walking with one arm around the other. The picture represents that no unresolved issues exist between them; all have been resolved and left on the path behind them.

Now change the picture and put an unresolved issue between them. That issue prevents them from walking closely next to each other, it separates them. Unresolved problems ultimately create physical and emotional separation that create pain and may even end in divorce.

It is your choice whether you continue as a Victim! If you want to stop making this Victim mistake, ask yourself:

- Am I bitter, holding grudges?
- Am I forgiving as I have been forgiven?
- Am I confessing when I was wrong?

Honest, objective answers to those questions will help you build rather than destroy relationships. Also, you should continue to check if you are playing the Victim by continuing to explore why you react a certain way in certain situations. If every time you talk to your sister and an old memory stirs in your heart, maybe you have not forgiven her, or you have something to confess.

Living as a victim probably hurts you more than it does others.

> When I kept silent, my bones grew old through my groaning all the day long. For day and night Your hand was heavy upon me; My vitality was turned into the drought of summer

Psalm 32:3-4, NKJV

God heals and restores people and their relationships through confession and forgiveness.

Reflections—Victim Scenario

As you review the following scenario, identify victim behaviors and make a note of how those behaviors trace back to the person's thinking. How might the relationship in the scenario be improved with the elimination of victim thinking?

Linda and Nicole have worked together at a Fortune 500 company for 15 years. Linda was a consultant who advised Nicole on the best sales practices for the field and helped Nicole advance to a corporate leadership position overseeing regional sales for the Southern United States. 10 years ago, Linda joined the company as a full-time employee working as a field sales manager and trainer.

Linda has performed so well that she advanced through the ranks and now leads the sales training organization at a national level. About 6 months ago, Linda got promoted to Senior Director of National Sales. Even though Linda and Nicole have worked together for a long time and are personal friends, when Linda got promoted, she did not hear from Nicole, which surprised her. She was angry that her friend did not congratulate her.

Linda has a higher corporate position than Nicole, but she and her team serve as internal consultants to regional sales leaders to understand and help them perform in the marketplace. The National Sales Meeting comes around each Fall, where internal and external speakers and trainers motivate and equip the salesforce. Linda sent Nicole an email telling her that she would be hiring a consultant to work with them on planning the meeting and securing the speakers.

Meanwhile, Nicole's boss asked her to plan the meeting, she did not mention to her boss what Linda said about hiring a consultant. So, she hired a consultant to help her complete the task. Some people at the corporate office and Linda heard that she hired a consultant. Many were shocked at this, given that budgets have been cut all-round due to shrinking sales and higher costs. Linda was particularly annoyed because she had already told Nicole that she had hired a consultant.

Linda went to Nicole's boss and explained that she had already hired a consultant who she had worked with before and was familiar with the organization. Linda convinced Nicole's boss that he should not allow Linda to hire another consultant. She explained that Nicole typically hired her friends as consultants and expected them to do her job for her.

Nicole heard this news from her boss in their weekly coaching meeting on Wednesdays at the end of the day. Nicole then left the office for the day. Her husband was out of town, so she got on a string of phone calls with sympathetic friends to share her plight.

The next day, Nicole decided she should defend herself against the naysayers.

Nicole invites another Regional Sales Director, Mario, to join her on a Zoom call to discuss the plans for the National Sales Meeting. Here's how the conversation goes.

"Thanks for joining me today to discuss plans for the meeting Mario. I appreciate your input," Nicole says as they kick off the Zoom meeting.

"My pleasure," Mario says brightly. "I'm glad to help."

Nicole starts the meeting by reviewing the agenda and speakers she has planned for the meeting. Mario is surprised that she has already planned everything since he thought she would be asking for his input.

When she finishes her review of the agenda, she asks, "So what did I miss? Are there other topics or speakers I should include, in your opinion?"

Mario replies, "I think you hit them all, I can't think of anything else. Have you checked in with Linda for her input?"

Nicole feels her face begin to turn flush at the question.

"Well no, I don't think I need her input. I've been here longer than she has. She just made friends with the right people to move up the ranks."

Mario noticed obvious irritation in Nicole's voice, and said, "That may be true, but she did implement some innovative practices that helped people in my Region quite a bit."

"Oh, of course it's true. I hired her as a consultant years ago. I was essentially her boss until she came on board full time. I don't know why I did not get promoted to her position. It's all politics."

Mario decided not to pursue the topic further and changed the subject.

They talked a few minutes longer, and Mario said, "Well it looks like you have it under control. Let me know if there's anything else I can do. I have another call in a few minutes."

"Thank you for your time, Mario," she said as she ended the Zoom.

Nicole picked up the phone and called her assistant, who was working from home that day.

"This is Marie," she answered.

"Hi Marie, how is your day going?" Nicole asked, feigning genuine concern.

"All is fine. I had to put out a few fires with the Arizona/New Mexico Area Manager, but I think everything is okay."

"That's great! I appreciate you so much! Hey, I need your help on something. I'm planning this National Sales Meeting, and I need some input from the field, outside of what Linda might say, because I think she's too wrapped up in politics," Nicole explained.

Marie answered with a little hesitancy based on Nicole's tone of voice. "Who do you need me to contact, and what do I need to find out?"

"I don't want to insult Linda, because she has gotten mad at me in the past for going around her. So why don't you tell people you are calling on behalf of the *Planning Committee* for the event. Call all the Regional Sales Directors and ask them, what in particular they want to see on the meeting agenda. That way Linda can't say I didn't ask the Field what they needed. Does that make sense?"

"Sure Nicole, I'll get on it this afternoon, after I finish the sales reports."

"Thank you! Please have this to me by Friday. I know that's only two days from now, but I know you can do this."

Marie thought to herself, "I'm going to have to work at night to get this done. But, oh well, what's new?"

"Sure Nicole, I'll get it done," she conceded. "I'll get back to you as soon as I can."

Nicole said, "You are a champ. You always come through for me!"

They traded good-byes and ended the call.

Scenario Questions

- Who is playing victim here?

_____

_____

_____

_____

- What happened that indicates that?

_____

_____

_____

_____

- What thinking needs to change to avoid playing the victim?

_____

_____

_____

- Do you see any elements of the Conflict Cycle? If you do, describe them below.

_____

_____

_____

- Reflecting on the scenario, what behaviors do you relate to? How can you change your thinking and behavior based on that?

_____

_____

_____

_____

REFLECTIVE QUESTIONS

- Do you find yourself doing any of the following?
  - ➢ Keep a detailed log of everything bad anyone has ever done to you. Read the list daily and pick at least two items to bring up that day.
  - ➢ Never live for today or hope for tomorrow. Only focus on how you have been mistreated in the past.
  - ➢ If you tire of thinking how you have been mistreated, think of all the bad things you did to others, and believe that others will never forgive you, or if they did, they did not mean it
  - ➢ Consume every day with what happened in the past, with *how it was*. Never tire of bringing up the same issue repeatedly, *ad nauseam*.

Describe specific times when you have acted in the above listed ways, including the people involved. Who do you need to forgive? Who do you need to make a confession to? This is a process, and it may take you some time to work through the list.

_____

_____

_____

_____

- Meditate on this scripture and remember how God and blessed you and always taken care of you.

  > *But recall the former days in which, after you were illuminated, you endured a great struggle with sufferings . . .*

  Hebrews 10:32, NKJV

- Meditate on and discuss the following quote from Dr. Fred Lybrand with your spouse.

  > *"Good marriages and relationships leave a trail of resolved issues."*

The Actor — Wear a Mask

Seeking and Sharing Truth

Acting can be fun. You can take on a persona different than your own. You can say and do things you would not if you were yourself. It can create some interesting experiences because you do not have to be the *real* you. Of course, that is why being an Actor in a relationship is such a crippling mistake – you are not being real!

The Actor role requires energy and work in a relationship because you act the way someone else wants you to act. You could be trying to think how someone else wants you to, or take on behavioral traits that really aren't the true you.

However you play out this mistake, you tell others what they want to hear, but you stay away from real issues, especially if it might expose who you *really* are. You are convinced that you must play this role, because you believe people around you would not tolerate your true self.

Above all, no one should ever see behind your mask. If that ever happens, life as you know it and all of your relationships would be over. If that looks like it might happen, your best tactic is to simply become what they want or change your mask to what others want to see. It's like a game of Hide-and-Seek, but the real you is never found. You can give them some information about you, but only information that supports who your character is at that time, which is often a lie. Never provide information that will allow people to see who you really are, what you really think or do.

You maintain control by keeping them thinking they know the real you. In fact, they would swear under oath they know who you are, but they do not. You control others by never giving anyone a reason to think that you are wearing a mask, which is the ultimate performance.

When you are an Actor in a relationship, you are not seeking or sharing the truth with people. For the Actor, relationships are not about the truth; they are solely about looking good to others! And, in spite of how it might look, the real audience is not the other people, it is you, the Actor.

Actors become experts at *walking on eggshells*. You know what that is like, right? When you are around specific people, you do not talk about certain things, because they will get upset. You prefer to relate and get along at the expense of truth.

With an Actor, something else happens, called a *conflict of values*. On the one hand, you may value truth. On the other, you value harmony or getting along.

So, you would assess any situation by thinking, "I don't want to upset them by sharing the truth or how I really feel about it. It's best to just ignore it to maintain a calmer atmosphere."

Your value of telling the truth comes in second to harmony, because you do not want emotional conflict. Your tendency then is to only tell them what they want to hear, not talk about *that*, dance around the problem, or to stay away from them. You will tend to act like everything is okay when it really is not.

Consider one sad implication of this behavior. You are free to lie, but not free to tell the truth. Lying or not sharing the truth can be easier than telling the truth. Be careful when you do not share the truth! Again, that happens most often when you value getting along more than sharing truth.

Another consequence is that others are not free to respond to you as they want, so you must manipulate and control them. In those situations, you may see or complain about how controlling and manipulative they are.

You might even say, "They don't want to talk about that huge problem, the 'elephant in the room.'"

Yet you rarely see your own controlling behavior. They are manipulating you by expressing anger, withholding affection, or a variety of other methods, to not talk about *that*. But you are manipulating back by not giving them the option to respond however they want. This is what is called the Control Boomerang.

This type of situation is a perfect illustration of how we teach people to lie. How does that work? Well, it is like training a dog. You already know how to do this, but here are some simple directions.

Suppose that you absolutely love the clothing you have on and you ask another person, "Do I look good in these clothes?"

You expect and want only one answer to that question, "Yes, absolutely!"

If you get a no, you can begin your training of them to get the right answer next time.

Again, Actors are not the only ones who exhibit this behavior, because all of the relationship mistakes and the Problem cause the ME strobe light to flash. When you are not interested in the truth or not willing to think of others more highly than yourself, you will tend to be defensive, discount what others say, and rationalize the way you are or act.

Being Real

So, are you an Actor, wearing a mask, not being real? Are you telling others what you think they want to hear? Are you less interested in truth than you are in your image, or the way people see you?

Being a real person takes much less energy. You will have energy for better things, like self-control, perseverance, and serving others. At first this may be tough because it requires openness and vulnerability. People will see both your strengths and weaknesses. On the upside they can utilize your strengths, help you with weaknesses and participate in growing a healthy relationship with you.

Being real is living God's way, as you can see in several places in scripture.

> *But, speaking the truth in love, [we] may grow up in all things into Him who is the head—Christ.*

> **Ephesians 4:15, NKJV**

*But exhort one another daily, while it is called
"Today," lest any of you be hardened through the
deceitfulness of sin.*

Hebrews 3:13, NKJV

You may see some traits of the Actor in your own
life. If you don't want to be an Actor, you can choose to
live differently. Ask yourself these questions:

- What truth am I not willing to seek or
  share?
- Am I being real with myself and others?
- Am I wearing a mask?

Your objective answer to those questions creates a
starting point for change. Remember that change will
not happen without the power of the Holy Spirit in
you. You are responsible to make the decision and He is
faithful to provide the power to fulfill the decision.

Reflections —Actor Scenario

Review the following scenario and look for clues
of Actor behavior. Think about the fact that this could
be you.

Molly and Greg have been married for only two
years. They both graduated from the same college
and decided to get married shortly after graduation.
Greg loves sports cars, nights on the town dancing

and amusement parks. His favorite food is Mexican food. Molly is more reserved and prefers to read in the evening or spend an afternoon under the trees in a park, her favorite food is a great smoothie or yogurt, and her favorite morning drink is Green Tea.

It's a lazy Saturday in the Fall and Greg hops out of bed early to fix Green Tea for Molly and himself. As he's walking to the room, he thinks to himself, "I would kill for a Starbuck's right now."

He brings the green tea in their room and asks Molly what she wants to do that day.

"Oh, I don't know, what were you thinking of doing?" she asks.

"Well, there a great event in the park, where we could go sit and listen to music and you read your book, I'll watch the people," he says with a smile.

She chuckles and asks, "You really want to go sit in the park? I was sure you would want to go down to the Fairgrounds where they are having an Auto Show."

"Nah, I'm kinda over that car phase. Parks are peaceful."

"Well okay, I can make us a picnic lunch," she says. "What do you want to eat?"

"Whatever you have handy. You know I'm not picky about that stuff."

A couple of hours pass, and they head out to the park. On the way out the door they run into their neighbors, James and Kelly Holmes. Molly and Kelly have become great friends in the last year. The couples have gone out for dinner several times, and the women always have fun, James seems to be having fun, but Greg feels out of place. James just wants to talk about his Financial Services business all the time, which Greg feels is over his head. To take care of that issue, Greg has been watching You Tube videos about retirement investments that are new to him.

Molly looks at Greg as if to ask, "Should we invite them to come with us?"

Greg nods his head enthusiastically and smiles.

She looks at Kelly and says, "Hey we are going down to the park for a few hours, do you want to join us?"

"Sure," Kelly answers. Then looks at James, and says, "That sounds like fun, doesn't it?"

James nods and says, "Yeah, that sounds good, we can run our errands another day." James calculates in his head the time lost sitting around in a park, instead of accomplishing what he planned that day. "Anything to keep her happy," he thinks to himself. She's the best thing that ever happened to me."

Kelly disappears inside the house to put together a picnic basket full of food. Molly follows her inside.

James says, "Greg, we can go sit on the porch for a few minutes. Can I get you a bottled water or something?"

"No" Greg replies, "I just finished one before we came out here. So what's your latest investment strategy?" he asks.

"Wow, I'm glad you asked. I just came up with a new innovative one."

James proceeds to describe the program in deep detail. Greg feigns interest and understanding or what makes absolutely no sense to him. James is winding up his explanation as their wives come out on the porch with their basket of goodies.

James says, "Why don't we take separate cars in case one of us has to leave earlier than the other?"

"Oh James," Kelly says, why in the world would one of us want to leave early? Why don't you drive?"

"Sure" he says. "Of course I want to show Greg and Molly our new SUV."

James climbs into the driver's seat and everyone piles in.

Molly says, "Greg, why don't you sit in the front with James. Kelly and I have some girl talk to tend to."

"Great! I'd love to see how this thing drives," he says as he jumps into the front seat.

They drive down to the park, where they spend four hours. Greg makes as much conversation as he can with James. He doesn't want him to know that he really doesn't understand investments, but he figures if he listens to him enough, he can at least figure out where to get some more information. By the time they leave the park, Greg's stomach is in knots. He thinks to himself, "I can't wait to get home and take a nap."

Molly looks over at him and asks, "Did you have fun today?"

"Of course!" he says enthusiastically as they all pile into James and Kelly's car. "I always love to get outdoors and relax on the weekends."

As they drive home, Greg makes small talk with James, hoping to avoid any talk about business or investments.

When they get home, Greg says to the group, "This was great! We should do this again sometime."

Kelly and Molly look at each other and giggle, and say almost in unison, "We're ready any time you are!"

Scenario Questions

- Who do you feel is an Actor in the scenario? (list one or more)

_____

_____

_____

_____

- What do you notice about their behavior or thinking that makes you think they are an Actor?

_____

_____

_____

_____

- How does being an Actor impact their relationships with others in the scenario?

_____

_____

_____

_____

- How might Actor behavior impact these marriages long term?

_____

_____

_____

_____

REFLECTIVE QUESTIONS

- Meditate on the below scriptures. What does Holy Spirit say to you about them? How would applying these scriptures impact your relationship with your spouse or friends?

  But, speaking the truth in love, [we] may grow up in all things into Him who is the head—Christ.

  Ephesians 4:15, NKJV

  But exhort one another daily, while it is called "Today," lest any of you be hardened through the deceitfulness of sin.

  Hebrews 3:13, NKJV

_____

_____

_____

_____

_____

_____

_____

_____

- Reflect on the questions below. And answer them honestly. Keep a journal over the next month, making a note of your answers to these questions.

  a. What truth am I not willing to seek or share?

  b. Am I being real with myself and others?

  c. Am I wearing a mask?

  _____

  _____

  _____

  _____

  _____

  _____

- Based on your journaling, write down some behaviors you need to change, and where you need help. Sometimes you will need professional help to overcome wearing a mask.

  _____

  _____

  _____

  _____

  _____

  _____

The Dictator

Have you ever tried to change somebody? Most likely you have.

Possibly you are thinking, "What is wrong with that?"

Maybe nothing is wrong with that, depending on who benefits the most with the change. Do you want them to change because it is best for them or because you could breathe a sigh of relief because they changed?

If you want someone to change for your benefit, this drives you to operate in fear, which then pushes you to manipulate or dominate them. In this case you may argue that they act in ways that harm them, their family, their friends and maybe even you, so they must change in order to stop the damage done or future damage. Notice the fear?

Two things will prevent your objectivity in this situation. First, you do not know the future, so you don't know that those behaviors will continue. Second, and most important, you are not operating in reality because change is the other person's decision, not yours. When you try to take control of something you cannot control, the other person's behavior, you've convinced yourself that you can control them, which is untrue.

No matter how perfectly you present them with objective truth, with passion, persuasion, subtlety or power, they still may not change. Why? The decision is theirs not yours. To understand this you must be objective and not follow your emotions. A barometer for your level of controlling is the level of emotion you have invested in the other person changing. This is a red flag to let you know that you are living the Dictator mistake.

Because I know and make the Dictator mistake, I have listed some mildly humorous representations of the Dictator's thinking, actions, and feelings.

Do you identify with any of the items listed below?

- Everyone must be the way you want them to be. You will entertain their thoughts, but ultimately, it is your decision on how they should think, act, and feel.

- You are committed to any control strategy necessary to change them, including manipulation and domination. If they do not, you will not have any peace or rest.

- You do not trust others to do something without your direction or input. If they got it right, it would be surprising. If they did do a good job, you would still have to make corrections, because they cannot do things as well as you can.

- You alone know what is best, and you proudly accept your role as a savior for those around you. Not only the savior, but you are also the Jr. Holy Spirit and their real conscience. You must convict them of what they are doing. You need to exert control to get them to act differently, because they will never change on their own.

- You always expect more and never tire of trying to change them; even if they are meeting your expectations. You always feel the need to raise the bar.
- You always look for what is wrong because the other person is not perfect like you.

These tendencies indicate that in the mind of the Dictator others should never be free to choose their own path because they will mess things up.

Solution for a Dictator

Fortunately, I studied under a brilliant mentor, Robert Fritz, who significantly impacted my life. I now understand grace better than I ever did before. Robert and his wife Rosalind helped me see my controlling behavior that indicated that I valued freedom for myself, not those around me. Below, I've listed some powerful quotes from Robert.

No one owes you anything in a relationship.

If you think someone owes you in a relationship, it becomes a Return on Investment (ROI) relationship.

What you give in the relationship requires that they return that investment with interest or treat you better than you treated them. If they don't return what you expect in the relationship you think they *owe* you something. Then you make demands on them to try to remove their freedoms to make them more like you want them to be. The fact is, even if you point out their awful behavior, it's their decision and choice to change their behavior. In a relationship consider these actions: hope, pray, encourage, and sometimes exhort and rebuke, but making them change is not your job. That is up to them and God.

When you cannot be yourself in a relationship, the relationship will become intolerable.

At first you may be able to tolerate this, but over time you will have the urge to get away. If you are controlling them, they will pull away in the same way that if they are controlling you, you will want to get away.

We all want to be free; when that is stifled through manipulation, domination or any other type of control, anyone will eventually want out. If you manipulate or dominate people, it can easily create a burning desire in them to be away from you. That's probably the opposite of what you want.

Relationships—Reality, Real Time, Real People

Effective relationships consist of two people not wearing masks, being real, spending time together, and resolving issues together. This gives the relationship the best chance to work.

Dr. Martin Howe referred to *touch, talk and time* as critical for relationships, especially marriages. Early in his counseling relationship with couples he requested that they begin each day talking with each other and ending the conversation by praying for each other. Those actions created a foundation for couples to know each other and be real.

It takes two to say "yes" and one to say "no."

Robert Fritz refers to this as the *math* of relationships. Trying to change a person is a common way to say *no* to a relationship. This means you are saying *yes* to the ideal person, but not the real person. Assume you want someone to stop wearing pink socks. Now you are saying *yes* to the non-pink sock person but no to the real person who wears pink socks. It doesn't mean the relationship is over, it's just an obstacle that creates separation between you and the other person. Saying *yes* accepts the bad with the good and is true reality.

Reflections—Dictator Scenario

Review the scenario below and look for clues of Dictator behavior and how they seem to be impacting the relationship. Think about what changes in thinking patterns that would help the Dictator in this scenario.

Mark and George live in the same community, which is near a large city. Both have spent countless hours working for the City Council free-of-charge. Mark is an entrepreneur and has owned a painting contracting business for 15 years. George has worked as a staff accountant in a Real Estate development firm for 20 years.

Mark constantly gets annoyed with George's *employee mindset.*

He often thinks to himself, "If I could only get George to be more innovative, I think we could make great changes for our neighborhood."

At a council meeting, the group is discussing changing guidelines regarding parked cars on the street in public areas. Currently, people are ticketed if a car is left sitting on the street longer than 2 days. The council is discussing extending this to five days. Here is the conversation.

George (addressing the board): "We need to stick to our by-laws. We cannot change how we do things without researching, polling our constituents, and thinking through consequences of any changes we make."

Mark grimaces and says, "They have elected us to make these decisions."

George says, "Yes, they have, but we have no data to substantiate that extending this to five days is safe."

Mark says, "We have policemen on beat in these areas. We hired them to keep us safe."

George acknowledges Mark's comment, then addresses the Council. "We have had an increase in crime in our area, and I believe we owe it to the people who elected us to determine what impact this might have on our community. While leaving a car parked on the street seems innocuous, our police force cannot be everywhere at once. My question to all of you is 'How do we know that it's safe for cars to be parked in public areas for longer than two days?'"

Several people on the Council squirm in their seats, noticing the conflict between the two leaders. Initially, when this Ordinance change was proposed for discussion, two others on the Council agree with George, and four agree with Mark.

The Council discusses the issue for 45 minutes, then determines that they do need to do more research before extending the time from 2-5 days.

As they leave the meeting, and go to the parking lot, Mark approaches George and says, "That was a good meeting."

"Yes, it was," George replies. "I'm glad the Council had the sense to see that times are different now for our small town. We can't just randomly change ordinances because we think it will be more convenient for visitors, or because one business, in this case the downtown condominium complex requests it."

Mark said, "I guess you are right."

George looks at his friend with a wry smile and says, "Of course I'm right."

Mark doesn't say anything but thinks to himself, "What a know-it-all. He's probably afraid of his own shadow. Our community is trying to create new opportunity and attract new business, I'm not sure this council is encouraging that."

They exchange pleasantries, then each return to their respective work places.

Scenario Questions

- Who in the story acts like a Dictator? What does the person say or do to indicate that?

_____

_____

_____

_____

_____

_____

_____

- How might that impact the relationships the person has with others?

  _____

  _____

  _____

  _____

  _____

- What do you notice about how the people around the Dictator respond? How does that impact relationships in the scenario?

  _____

  _____

  _____

  _____

  _____

  _____

- What could the Dictator do differently?

  _____

  _____

  _____

  _____

  _____

  _____

- Give specific examples of any other mistake(s) you see.

_____

_____

_____

_____

_____

_____

REFLECTIVE QUESTIONS

- Do you notice yourself in the scenario? If so, how might you change based on what you read in the scenario.

_____

_____

_____

_____

- If you are like the Dictator in the scenario, how do people around you react? How do you think that is impacting relationships?

_____

_____

_____

_____

- What stood out to you in the scenario, that you can learn from?

_____

_____

_____

_____

Exercise

- Think of any close relationship with have. Think of the other person and identify three changes you would like them to make, then rank them in order of importance.

CHANGE YOU WOULD LIKE THEM TO MAKE	RANK

- Choose the item you rank as most important and continue to ask yourself *Why* five times in a row.

  For example, assume the desired change is, "I want James to call me at least once every day."

  1. Why? Because that is what friends should do.
  2. Why should friends do that? Because it shows they care.
  3. Why should friends show they care? Because friendship should not be taken for granted.
  4. Why should friendships not be taken for granted? Because friendship is precious.
  5. Why is friendship precious? Because our friends can help us through difficult times.
  6. What did you notice from doing this exercise?

- What emotions did you find tied up in the change you want them to make?

- Who would benefit most from the change you want them to make?

- What did you discover about your own Dictator behavior from this exercise?

- What should you change or continue doing when you think about what you want others to do? For example, continue to or start to think about who benefits most from the change you want the other person to make.

REFLECTIVE QUESTIONS

- How can you engage others to give you feedback about your behavior that you may not be aware of?

_____

_____

_____

_____

- Why does God want your thinking aligned with truth?

_____

_____

_____

_____

- Do you personally operate based on truth, or opinions, speculations, and guesses?

_____

_____

_____

_____

_____

- Notice when you make statements as though they were facts, and they are not based on the truth. Start to make a change.

_____

_____

_____

_____

_____

- Do you live in the past and act like a victim?

_____

_____

_____

_____

_____

_____

- If you do act like a victim, what can you do to change it?

_____

_____

_____

_____

_____

_____

- Do you wear a mask to protect people from seeing the real you?

_____

_____

_____

_____

_____

- How would relationships be improved if you took the mask off?

_____

_____

_____

_____

_____

_____

- Do you try to change people to make them act the way you want them to act?

_____

_____

_____

_____

_____

_____

- Do you find yourself judging people because they don't act the way you think they should? What would happen if you let go of judgment and allowed people to be who they are?

_____

_____

_____

_____

_____

_____

PATH OF LEAST RESISTANCE

The Problem creates a Path of Least Resistance. Let's start by examining the three areas of sin, desire, and ME. These are the foundation to creating a path of least resistance, which does not have a good ending.

Sin, Desires, and ME

Sin

> *The doctrine of original sin seems an offense to reason, but once accepted it makes total sense of the of the entire human condition.*
>
> **Blaise Pascal, French Religious**
> **Philosopher and Scientist**

What a profound statement! Unfortunately, the statement is only profound to those who trust God and His Word. The truth is, God allowed the original sin to infect all of mankind. We are all born into sin. God's grace and His Holy Spirit are the only things that prevent the evil from being more prevalent in our world.

You have the same options of evil available to you as Hitler and Adam and Eve. It all starts with the temptation to do something God stated would be bad for you. The path remains the same until God changes it.

Read the quote below and think about your own past actions or past sins. If you are honest with yourself, you can identify with these words.

> *The history of every temptation, and of every sin,*
> *is the same; the outward object of attraction,*
> *the inward commotion of mind, the increase*
> *and triumph of passionate desire; ending in the*
> *degradation, slavery, and ruin of the soul.*
>
> **Jamieson, R., Fausset**[2]

Your sin nature, which is like an *autopilot,* will make that quote a consistent story for your life if you do not make a deliberate choice to walk with the Lord and choose His answers.

Desires

When you study the account of Adam and Eve's sin in the Garden of Eden and apply it to your life, you will see that the object of attraction, eventually leads to triumph of passionate desire. You are the culprit, not Satan, because you are the one who chooses your actions. If Satan was the culprit he would be the only one suffering consequences. You suffer from the consequences of Adam and Eve's sin and your sin nature. You and others around you will suffer the consequences of your current sin.

Robert Fritz breaks this desire into three separate categories to help us understand how to create. You can apply this wisdom toward making better choices. You can understand desire through the analogy of a camera lens. You can zoom in for a close shot, zoom out for a long shot or broad picture, or use a medium shot to capture essential items and perspective.

Think of your current desires, then compare them to the table below.

Appetites, impulses and pleasures (close shot)	Values and aspirations (medium shot)	Vague hopes and longings (long shot)
Very short time frame, instant gratification required	A sense of what is and is not important	Someday it will happen
Generally self-absorbed, self-serving	Essential organizing principles in life	Wishful thinking, "If I could win the lottery"
If resolution is not quick, most likely will be abandoned	Values that help create priorities for your life	Time frame is long and indeterminate
	Clear purposes, goals, and objectives	Thoughts and ideas are far away, fuzzy, and out of focus

If any of your desires do not fit the Medium Shot, then expect problems. The Close Shot describes many temptations and even sin. You can see in Genesis 3:6 and 1 John 2:16 that sin seems to have closer ties to the physical, temporal part of man.

> *So when the woman saw that the tree was good for food, that it was pleasant to the eyes, and a tree desirable to make one wise, she took of its fruit and ate. She also gave to her husband with her, and he ate.*
>
> **Genesis 3:6, NKJV**

> *For all that is in the world—the lust of the flesh, the lust of the eyes, and the pride of life—is not of the Father but is of the world.*
>
> **1 John 2:16, NKJV**

Not all appetites, impulses, and pleasures are wrong. God created things for our pleasure, created us with the ability to experience appetites, impulses, and pleasures, and generally, you can consider them as neutral. Your sin nature focuses you on these pleasures and turns you into a slave to the pleasures.

ME

What makes your *Close Shot* of Appetites, Impulses and Pleasures so powerful? The focus is on ME! It encourages you to become self-absorbed and creates a path of least resistance to the Problem, making everything about ME.

When you are following your appetites, impulses, and pleasures your answer to any conviction is, "The Bible may say that, but I don't see it like that."

Its heartbeat, breath, and cry are all, "ME, ME, ME, Self, Self, Self, I, I, I!"

This is the disease of *the Flashing ME*. When you think everything revolves around you, Satan's strategy to get you to question God's Word, will work on you more easily. That is what he did with Adam and Eve. He has been using this strategy on mankind from the beginning.

. . . for he is a liar and the father of it.

John 8:44, NKJV

When you become entangled in questioning God, your only other option is to trust something other than God, which most often means yourself. Self-dependence makes you blind to the truth by pursuing your own way and deceives you into thinking that this is not sin. Self-dependence if fertile ground for going down the wrong path.

For all that is in the world—
the lust of the flesh, the lust of the eyes,
and the pride of life—is not of the Father but
is of the world.

1 John 2:16, NKJV

You may say, "God will forgive me anyway."

If you are a child of God, this is true, and He will also allow you to suffer the consequences of your sinful choice!

Look at the graph below and you can see how the underpinnings of Sin, Desire, and ME create a path that glorifies your ME rather than God. Essentially, this is idolatry and the idol being worshipped is *ME*!

Because you make everything about ME, you demonstrate that your primary desire is to satisfy ME now! That thinking drives you to want what God prohibits, to gratify your senses and look good to everyone. Now! This is your natural tendency, as the Bible shows us.

Hell (Death) and Destruction are never full; So the eyes of man are never satisfied.

Proverbs 27:20, NKJV

For where envy and self-seeking exist, confusion and every evil thing are there.

James 3:16, NKJV

Fear drives all of this; fear that you won't get what you want or what you think is best for you versus what God *knows* is best for you. Satan uses this strategy the same way he tries to plant doubt of God's goodness in your mind.

"Did God really say . . . ?"

The Problem's Path of Least Resistance

When you constantly entertain your ME or act like a baby, your behavior becomes driven by the *Problem* structure. You will find yourself on the Path of Least

Resistance, fulfilling your ME thoughts and desires. "Where you look, you tend to go," so you end up taking actions like those listed below.

- DEPEND on self, live self-sufficient, ignore truth and standards, engage in poor thinking, disruptive emotions, because *it feels right.*
- LOVE me and seek my best, in pursuit of *the lust of eyes, lust of the flesh, and the pride of life.*
- LIVE daily in my Judgment, men try to control work and activities, women try to control relationships.

Clearly, these actions ultimately will destroy any kind of relationship you are in.

<u>REFLECTIVE QUESTIONS</u>

- How does original sin relate to the entire human condition?

_____

_____

_____

_____

- What are the three main categories of your desires? How do you see those playing out in your life right now? How do they hinder and enhance your relationship with God?

_____

_____

_____

_____

- How is your ME currently getting in the way of relationships?

_____

_____

_____

_____

- Think about ways that you depend on yourself, love yourself and seek your best, and judge others. How would relationships with God and others improve if you focused on pursuing the best for others?

_____

_____

_____

_____

IT STARTED IN THE GARDEN

This whole issue with the Path of Least Resistance started in the Garden of Eden when the serpent enticed Eve to eat the forbidden fruit. Instead of relying on God's promises and following His one command not to eat of the fruit of the Tree of Life, she chose to take a *ME* action and eat the delicious-looking fruit now. Let's look at the results of this for the serpent, Adam, and Eve. Here's God's reaction.

> *So the LORD God said to the serpent:*
> *"Because you have done this, You are cursed*
> *more than all cattle,*
> *And more than every beast of the field;*
> *On your belly you shall go,*
> *And you shall eat dust*
> *All the days of your life. And I will put*
> *enmity*
> *Between you and the woman,*
> *And between your seed and her Seed;*
> *He shall bruise your head,*
> *And you shall bruise His heel."*

To the woman He said:
"I will greatly multiply your sorrow and
your conception;
In pain you shall bring forth children;
Your desire shall be [e]for your husband,
And he shall rule over you."
Then to Adam He said, "Because you have
heeded the voice of your wife, and have
eaten from the tree of which I commanded
you, saying, 'You shall not eat of it':
"Cursed is the ground for your sake;
In toil you shall eat of it
All the days of your life.
Both thorns and thistles it shall [f]bring
forth for you,
And you shall eat the herb of the field.
In the sweat of your face you shall eat bread
Till you return to the ground,
For out of it you were taken;
For dust you are,
And to dust you shall return."

Genesis 3:14-19, NKJV

Adam and Eve's sin of disobedience, following their *now* desire for delicious fruit and relying on their own judgment or self-sufficiency and ME, changed the situation for all mankind. Let's look more closely at the characters in this saga.

Here's a chart showing what Satan did and didn't do.

Observations about Satan

Observations about Satan	
DID	**DIDN'T**
Ask one question, "Has God indeed said..."	Tell her to eat
Made one statement, "You will not surely die."	Offer the fruit to her
Imply God lied to them	Pick the fruit for her
Imply that God had a secret	Put the fruit on her lips
Imply they could be like God	Force her to eat the fruit
Deceive Eve to depend on someone or something other than God	
Introduce the opportunity or temptation to sin	

REFLECTIVE QUESTIONS

- What correlations do you see between what Satan did and how Eve followed the Path of Least Resistance?

_____

_____

_____

_____

- Who was glorified in this situation?

_____

_____

_____

_____

- How did that ultimately impact her relationship with God?

_____

_____

_____

_____

_____

_____

- Identify three doubts you have related to your current circumstances. See if you can find scriptures that God has stated to deal with them. Here is one to help you get started, Philippians 4:6.

_____

_____

_____

_____

_____

Observations about Eve

Review the chart below regarding what Eve did and didn't do.

Observations about Eve	
DID	DIDN'T
Converse with the serpent	Question whether what the serpent said was wrong
Depend on her opinion rather than God	Question her understanding of the serpent's claims
Believe the serpent's claims	Ask Adam or God if the serpent's claims were correct
Decide the fruit was good for food, pleasant to the eyes and would make her wise	Ask God or Adam about the serpent's questions
Give the fruit to Adam	Check with Adam before eating, "Adam, is this okay?"

REFLECTIVE QUESTIONS

- How did Eve's actions demonstrate self-sufficiency?

_____

_____

_____

_____

- How does what she did compare to how you act in your daily life?

_____

_____

_____

_____

_____

- How did Eve's actions damage her relationship with Adam and with God?

_____

_____

_____

_____

_____

Observations about Adam

How did Adam act in this situation? Let's take a look.

Observations about Adam	
DID	**DIDN'T**
Depended on and obeyed Eve's opinion rather than God	Tell Eve what she did was wrong
Ignore God's command, and God's Word, which was given to him before Eve was created	Talk to God about what Eve did
Take the fruit	Talk to God about what he was about to do
Eat the fruit	If present, he did not • Enter the conversation • Correct the misquoted command • Check with God about Satan's claims • Check with God before they did anything

REFLECTIVE QUESTIONS

- What verse in Genesis 3 tells you that Adam depended on Eve?

_____

_____

_____

_____

- In that same verse what did God do to Adam and all men after him?

_____

_____

_____

_____

- Identify some information sources or people who you might listen to more than God.

_____

_____

_____

_____

_____

Observations about God

How did God act in this situation? Here's what He did and didn't do.

Observations about God	
DID	**DIDN'T**
Allow Eve to talk with Satan	Stop the temptation
Allow Eve to be deceived	Stop the sin
Allow Eve and Adam to choose to disobey	Tell them they could have a second chance
Seek them after they sinned	Ignore the consequences He had stated to them regarding eating the fruit from one particular tree
Maintain a relationship with them	*Disown* them or say He was going to create some better people
Show mercy and love by providing a solution for their sin	
Show justice by initiating consequences	
Shut the gate to the Garden, Open the door to Heaven	

REFLECTIVE QUESTIONS

- What choices did God allow Adam and Eve to make?

_____

_____

_____

_____

_____

- How did He show Himself as a loving father?

_____

_____

_____

_____

_____

- How can God's actions change all your relationships?

_____

_____

_____

_____

_____

Your Current Garden

As you can see, you can correlate what happened in the Garden to your own life and current relationships. The original sin is not something that happened long ago and far, far away. It relates to your default behaviors, how you operate in relationship with others, and your relationship with God.

If people in the world continue to focus on ME, as is natural, and choose not to focus on God, the future is bleak for relationships. The good news is you can choose to focus on God. It takes simple dependence on the perfection of God. Every circumstance in life is an opportunity to trust God, or trust yourself, or something other than God. You will either follow your sin nature and flash your ME or reflect Christ's image.

Remember, you are probably flashing your ME in those times you have negative emotions like anger, irritability, discouragement, or disappointment. Those are excellent times to realize you are not trusting God's perfection in your current circumstance. I have found that is a simple way to see that I am walking in my flesh and not with God.

<u>REFLECTIVE QUESTIONS</u>

- Who was responsible for Eve's behavior in the Garden of Eden?

_____

_____

_____

_____

_____

- How did her actions show rebellion to God?

_____

_____

_____

_____

_____

- Who did Adam obey when he ate the forbidden fruit? What should he have done differently?

_____

_____

_____

_____

_____

- What did God allow to happen in the Garden scenario?

  _____

  _____

  _____

  _____

  _____

- What did God do after they rebelled toward Him?

  _____

  _____

  _____

  _____

  _____

A BLEAK FUTURE FOR RELATIONSHIPS

God clearly revealed the consequences of choosing a life that depends on something or someone other than Him. Throughout the Word of God, you can find stories of disastrous consequences when people chose to trust themselves and their own judgment. By contrast, the Word of God also recounts many stories of those who were blessed by following God and trusting Him.

Look at King David, who chose to have an affair with his neighbor, then sent her husband to the frontlines of war so he would perish. David suffered many consequences for many years after that.

By contrast, Abram (who became Abraham) had a very different outcome than King David. He left a posh life in Ur, the center of culture opulence in his day, to go out into the wilderness and father a people. Abram wasn't given a strategic plan and a roadmap, but he trusted God and what He told him to do.

The Future of Relationships

Given that many people are not following what God wants, relationships are suffering and will continue to suffer. One of the most severe consequences for you and your family is clearly outlined in Exodus.

> *. . . For I, the LORD your God, am a jealous God, visiting the iniquity of the fathers upon the children to the third and fourth generations of those who hate Me*

Exodus 20:5, NKJV

In spite of the clarity of God's warning in Exodus, people ignore it and therefore families throughout the world suffer the consequences. Here's an excerpt from John MacArthur's book, *The Fulfilled Family* that explains this further.

> *Each year several million couples pledge themselves in marriage, vowing to love each other for better or worse. But many of those marriages will end in divorce. That contributes to the problem of unwanted children. There are as many abortions by married women as non-married. Couples often do not want children. One-third of all couples in their child-bearing years have been sterilized. Why? Because children*

interfere with divorce. If you do not have children, you can leave easier. Children get in the way.

We have a generation of children growing up in families that are in chaos. Many children are saying to themselves, 'The last thing I want to do is get married. I don't want to repeat this mess.' They have lived in chaotic and totally unfulfilled families, so they don't want anything to do with marriage. But they want to fulfill their sex drives, so they go from person to person with no commitment. The next generation may never get married.

Even marriages that do hang together are often characterized by adultery, unfaithfulness, lying, cheating, loss of respect, loss of trust, pride, self-centeredness, materialism, laziness, and loneliness. Our nation is a mess, but the sad thing is that those characteristics have crept into the church. Believers are having marital problems, too.

The answer is not more counselors, more marriage seminars, or more books on marriage; the answer is in Ephesians 5:18: 'Be filled with the Holy Spirit.' When that is accomplished,

> *God Himself will produce the virtues that make*
> *for a meaningful marriage. People are good at*
> *patching up symptoms but not so good at dealing*
> *with reality. What we need to do is back up and*
> *look at God's principles.* [3]

Please do not let pain from your family system control your life, depress you, or make you a victim. In other words, don't let your ME take control. Instead, consider the hope God provides.

> *. . . but showing mercy to thousands, to those who*
> *love Me and keep My commandments.*

Exodus 20:6, NKJV

God's Statement of the Future of Relationships

God has provided clear direction for us to follow to put hope back into relationships and has forecast where relationships will go in the future if people do not listen to Him.

The renowned psychologist Carl Rogers stated, "It would take a bolder man than me to predict what will emerge (for relationships and marriage)."

That statement accurately describes any human trusting in one's own knowledge, because no one can see the future. Interestingly, Rogers made that statement even though his basic premise is that people are inherently good and seek to make things better.

When you trust God, you don't need to predict the future, because God tells you what to expect. God lists a number of current problems that destroy relationships.

> *But know this, that in the last days perilous times will come: For men will be lovers of themselves, lovers of money, boasters, proud, blasphemers, disobedient to parents, unthankful, unholy, unloving, unforgiving, slanderers, without self-control, brutal, despisers of good, traitors, headstrong, haughty, lovers of pleasure rather than lovers of God, having a form of godliness but denying its power. And from such people turn away! For of this sort are those who creep into households and make captives of gullible women loaded down with sins, led away by various lusts… But evil men and impostors will grow worse and worse, deceived and being deceived.*

2 Timothy 3:1-6, 13, NKJV

The issues described in 2 Timothy have been with us since sin entered the world, and they continue to worsen. The ruler of the world, Satan, uses those characteristics listed to incite our flesh to act *independent* of God and each other. Let's look at reasons that relationships will get worse if we don't turn to God.

Four Reasons Relationships Will Get Worse

While many issues and situations can impact relationships, here, we will explore four key reasons.

Self-Love

For men will be lovers of themselves, lovers of money, boasters, proud, blasphemers . . .

2 Timothy 3:2, NKJV

These type of people are self-centered, self-absorbed, self-indulgent, and self-satisfied. Everything is about them and what they can get. Sometimes they appear to be focused on others, but ultimately, they are focused on how they will benefit. Self-love is the root cause of relational problems and often leads to the other four reasons relationships will get worse. Satan wants you to focus on yourself because that means you are not focused on God.

God esteems humility. Think about the fruit of the Spirit.

But the fruit of the Spirit is love, joy, peace, longsuffering, kindness, goodness, faithfulness, gentleness, self-control. Against such there is no law.

Galatians 5:22-23, NKJV

Self-control in the above scripture is specifically directed at self-love, if not all the fruit of the Spirit mentioned. More directly look at God's warning through James.

> *For where envy and self-seeking exist, confusion and every evil thing are there.*

James 3:16, NKJV

God places a high value on humility. Jesus modeled humility and serving others as the example to follow.

> *Let nothing be done through selfish ambition or conceit, but in lowliness of mind let each esteem others better than himself. Let each of you look out not only for his own interests but also for the interests of others.*

Philippians 2:3-4, NKJV

Humbling yourself is the path to God's grace and care. Only then will you see how needy and sinful you are. Only then will you see God's abundant goodness and holiness, and only then will you cast your cares on Him. Thinking about ME may not be always bad, but here's the test. Is your behavior self-controlled or self-absorbed? If you rely on the Holy Spirit, you will likely be able to tell the difference. Let's look at Matthew for guidance.

You shall love the Lord your God . . .
You shall love your neighbor as yourself.

Matthew 22:37, 39

Using these verses as a guide, you can see that when your ME does not interfere with obeying God and loving, or pursuing the best for others, then your ME thoughts, actions or feelings are okay and acceptable to God. Notice that **obeying** God is a clearer measure of what it means to love God.

Many people will say they love God and mean it, but the true test is will you obey Him, even when He asks you do things you may not want to do.

If you love Me, keep My commandments.

John 14:15, NKJV

You demonstrate your love for God when you obey Him.

How do you test whether you are loving others by *pursuing their best?* If you focus on what others should be doing, it most often turns into being judgmental.

When you hear yourself thinking, "They should be helping me, but they are too selfish," your ME is flashing. When you love someone, pursuing their best means you do not require that they make changes to their life or behavior, and it's okay if they do not help you. Rather than focusing on your expectations of them, you focus on God's expectations of you.

Rebellion in the Family

The Bible speaks of perilous times and perilous men (mankind) and what we will see.

. . . disobedient to parents . . .

2 Timothy 3:2, NKJV

This statement is an indictment of both children and the parents. In a household where parents are self-absorbed, children are impacted. When parents are caught up in themselves, children do not see a model of serving others, loving others, and submitting to authority. While a child understands the role of authority, their built-in desire for freedom, combined with their sin nature, will view authority as repressive rather than protective.

With a distorted view of parental authority, children are disobedient, hold little respect for others, and grow up with a skewed view of all authority.

All this is driven by the real Problem, which is thinking, "It's all about ME."

John MacArthur explains part of the problem with understanding the role of parents in the world:

Disobedience to parents is part of the problem,
but with day-care centers, separations of families,
and so forth, it is difficult for children to
comprehend what a parent is and what their role
is supposed to be.

Lack of Familial Love

Another way Timothy describes perilous times is

. . . unloving . . .

2 Timothy 3:3, NKJV

The Greek word used for unloving means, *without natural affection or family love.* If self-love is a catalyst for the list of abhorrent traits listed in 2 Timothy, then it consumes any energy available for others and begrudges any affection bestowed on others, because it does not see beyond itself. People who are absorbed with self-love are not interested in others unless they stand to gain something.

Headlines are brimming with stories of murder, abuse, and awful events in families. Even if your reaction to a family member was gritting your teeth wishing they would leave you alone, or you show contempt for a family member you say you love, you can see lack of familial love. God's Word often uses the family as a picture of how God deals with us and how we treat each other. You understand the picture because protecting and caring for family is natural and not doing that is unnatural.

Attacks Directed Against the Home

> *For this sort are they who creep into houses,*
> *and lead captive silly women laden with sins,*
> *led away in various lusts . . .*

2 Timothy 3:6, NKJV

At the time this was written, women had been tightly controlled, as you could observe in countries ruled by Islam. Many women had not been allowed to ask questions and learn, so they were easy targets of false teachers. Despite women being free to learn today, they will still be targets of false teachers because of their relational design.

God does not indict women to say they are *silly* and *laden with sins*. The emphasis is on the contrast to sensible, wise women. Here's what John MacArthur says about the matter.

> *The home is going to become fair game for every*
> *con man and sexual pervert. It's all going to come*
> *crashing down on the home, God's basic unit of*
> *human society.*

The idea of "creep into houses" is like a burglar sneaking in to steal. Here the false teacher creeps in to "steal" truth and corrupt the minds of those in the household. This passage speaks about women mainly because that was happening in Ephesus. Therefore, those women listening to the false teachers are not only "loaded down with sins, led away by various lusts" in their homes, but also impacting the church.

Moral deficiency, deception, and false teachers are linked. This is the common repetition of the story in the Garden of Eden. Self-love weakens you, driving you to seek temporary satisfaction of your appetites, impulses, and pleasures rather than the satisfaction of eternal rewards. When your ME is flashing, it promotes a desire for something other than God and leaves you with a burden of sin and shame. It blinds you to wisdom and reality.

The Next Generation

To shape the future of relationships you must ask what you are passing on to the next generation. What do your children and your grandchildren see in you? That is what they will emulate as they grow up. Are you allowing your Flashing ME to cause you to be self-centered and self-absorbed? Or by contrast are you demonstrating a *pursuing-their-best* attitude, where you put others first?

Is your ultimate focus to please and pursue God, or please and pursue your own desires? What would your life be like if you pursued God's desires for you, your spouse and your family rather than trying to please yourself and get what you think you need?

The next generation is the hope for the future! What you demonstrate to them through your relationship with God and other people will impact the world for years to come!

REFLECTIVE QUESTIONS

- Meditate on this scripture, then write down how you believe it impacts your family. How will it impact your actions?

  . . . For I, the LORD your God, am a jealous God, visiting the iniquity of the fathers upon the children to the third and fourth generations of those who hate Me

  Exodus 20:5, NKJV

  _____

  _____

  _____

  _____

- Meditate on the below scripture. Pick just one of those nine elements and identify at least three ways it would make your relationships better.

  But the fruit of the Spirit is love, joy, peace, longsuffering, kindness, goodness, faithfulness, gentleness, self-control. Against such there is no law.

  Galatians 5:22-23, NKJV

_____

_____

_____

_____

_____

- What examples do you see of rebellion to authority in your family? How could more freedom help reduce rebellion? Would freedom be more in line with pursuing their best?

_____

_____

_____

_____

_____

- How can you increase familial love in your family?

_____

_____

_____

_____

_____

_____

- How can you defend against attacks directed against your home?

_____

_____

_____

_____

- For marriages, what are you doing that does not align with the roles God ordained for husbands and wives in Ephesians 5:22-33?

_____

_____

_____

_____

_____

- What are some examples in the Bible where people trusted their own judgment and got into trouble?

_____

_____

_____

_____

_____

_____

• What are some examples in the Bible of people who trusted in God and obeyed Him without question and ended up with positive results?

_____

_____

_____

_____

_____

_____

CREATING THE RELATIONSHIPS YOU WANT

We have looked at the Problem and four mistakes that destroy relationships. These should have made you aware of how you act in a relationship and the damage it can cause. At GR8 Relationships we are about teaching you how to grow, preserve and nurture relationships! Let's shift our focus to three overarching problems I see repeatedly in relationships.

Three Common Problems

In my many years of working with people, I find that three problems show up often. Certainly, more than three problems exist, but these three capture the struggle I observe in relationships. I describe them as: rudderless, blind, and unfocused.

Rudderless

Rudderless means a lack of clarity about purpose strategy and goals. If you are unclear about where you are going, the following question describes you.

"What is the difference between a ship without a rudder and a captain without a charted course?"

Nothing! Both will go *somewhere* driven by the currents, wind, and tide. Is that you?

Blind

Perhaps you are blind. You could be out of touch with reality, or how things really are. The state of your life is unclear. When you are unclear about your current reality, you tend to fall into two fallacies. One is believing that things are *better* than they really are, or *worse* than they really are. You become subjective rather than objective about life. You editorialize, estimate, guess and speculate rather than observe reality.

Unfocused

This is most often a result of being rudderless and blind, but it can also happen by ignoring a clear end-result and current reality. When you are unfocused, your days, weeks, and months are filled with inconsistent and uncoordinated actions. You are constantly *fighting brush fires*. You may be remarkably busy with few results to show for your efforts.

Solution: There-Here-Path (THP)

So, where there's a problem, there is always a solution. At GR8 Relationships we talk about THP, which stands for There-Here-Path. THERE stands for the future, "I want to go There." HERE represents the present, ". . . but I am Here." The PATH represents the Transition, "That looks like the Path I could take."

THP is the beginning of the Creative Process that Robert Fritz teaches. The process has been around for thousands of years and is the foundation for most things created or done. Your brain is wired for THP and now you can become disciplined to follow the process.

The quote below from Abraham Lincoln demonstrates the THP structure.

If we could first know there we are, and wither
we are tending, we could better judge what to do,
and how to do it.

Get yourself focused by first determining your THERE, then your HERE, and finally develop some actions to move you along the PATH. You must be intentional in the PATH, because if you are not you will follow the path of least resistance we described earlier, which ultimately leads to the destruction of relationships.

REFLECTIVE QUESTIONS

- Do you relate to the descriptions of Rudderless, Blind, or Unfocused? Are you rudderless? What can you do to change that? How can you engage others around you to help identify these issues if you have a blind spot?

_____

_____

_____

_____

_____

- Reflect on this quote by Abraham Lincoln. How can you apply it to your life?

    If we could first know there we are, and wither we are tending, we could better judge what to do, and how to do it.

_____

_____

_____

_____

_____

- Are you out of touch with reality? What can you
  do to change that?

_____

_____

_____

_____

_____

- Are you constantly fighting brush fires? What
  can you do to change that?

_____

_____

_____

_____

_____

STUDY GUIDE

Scripture Meditation

Time: 30 minutes a day

Each day read and meditate on one of the scriptures listed below, or as directed by your session leader.

Follow these steps:

1. Get in a quiet place without distraction.
2. Play a praise song and just listen to the words.
3. Ask God to reveal His heart and meaning to you as you read the scriptures.
4. Write your reflections below or in your journal.
5. Read the scriptures daily so you receive maximum revelation.

Romans 6:13, NKJV	Proverbs 3:5-5, NKJV	2 Peter 1:3, NKJV
Hebrews 10:32, NKJV	Ephesians 4:15, NKJV	Hebrews 3:13, NKJV
James 3:16, NKJV	Exodus 20:6, NKJV	2 Timothy 3:2, NKJV
Phillipians 2:3-4, NKJV	John 14:15, NKJV	2 Timothy 3:6, NKJV

REFLECTIVE QUESTIONS

- How will understanding the concept of *The Flashing Me* impact your relationships with others in a positive way?

_____

_____

_____

_____

- Do you identify most with the Politician, Actor, Victim or Dictator? How has this impacted your relationships in a negative way?

_____

_____

_____

_____

- Are you rebelling against God in some way? How is that impacting your relationship with Him and others around you?

_____

_____

_____

_____

- How are the issues of rudderless, blind, or unfocused impacting you? What do you need to change to make the most of your relationships?

_____

_____

_____

_____

- What four key reasons relationships will get worse in the world we live in? How do you see these playing out in your own life? What can you do to change the trend?

_____

_____

_____

_____

TOOLS

The following tools will enable you to understand yourself, your spouse, and how you can work together to handle conflict. The videos listed below are a part of the FREE video course that corresponds to the information in this book. Completing all the courses will be instrumental for you to find FREEDOM!

You can find all these tools (and many more) on our website www.GR8relate.com at the TOOLS tab.

Kolbe Assessment https://gr8relate.com/kolbe

You can trust the validity and accuracy of the Kolbe instrument to show you your strengths and instincts. The Kolbe also helps you easily see and understand how the strengths and talents of one person may not be considered as strengths by another. This critical information will help you bridge the gap between reality and your expectations of them. Once you complete the assessment, you will receive detailed reports that will help you understand your strengths and talents and how to use your strengths in a complementary way with your spouse, family member, or friend's strengths. By understanding your instincts you can more easily discuss your differences, laugh about them, and develop ways to deal with them.

The *Thomas-Kilman Conflict Mode Instrument* (TKI)   https://gr8relate.com/tki

The TKI is the world's best-selling instrument for understanding conflict. It helps you see that conflict can be beneficial and useful, instead of thinking conflict as bad. You will be provided detailed information on effectively using all five conflict modes: competing, collaborating, compromising, avoiding, and accommodating.

The *Fundamental Interpersonal Relations Orientation-Behavior* ™ (FIRO-B®). https://gr8relate.com/firob

The FIRO-B helps you understand how you interact at work and personal life. This easy-to-complete-assessment will provide critical insights into how an individual interacts with others. This personality instrument measures how you typically behave with others and how you expect them to act toward you.

Individual Videos

We have a FREE video course that corresponds with the information in this book.

These are short courses that you can watch/listen at your own pace. Enter the information in parenthesis below into your browser and you will be taken to a video course. When you are online, scroll down and click the "Sign Up / Start Course" button to create an account. You only need an account to access all the free courses.

There are two options:

- BOOK SERIES Courses: Each book in the GR8 Relationships series will have a video course with specific videos selected from the COMPLETE Courses that help explain the contents of the book. This book's video course is below.
  - *The Problem That Destroys Relationships* (https://gr8relate.com/video-courses/the-problem-that-destroys-relationships/)
- COMPLETE Courses: These are the original, complete courses that give you more details about the information in this book.
  - 05A - The PROBLEM and 4 Mistakes That Damage Relationships (https://gr8relate.com/video-courses/

problem-and-4-mistakes-that-damage-relationships/)

- 05B - The PROBLEM Creates a Path to Bad Relationships (https://gr8relate.com/video-courses/problem-creates-path-to-bad-relationships/)
- 05C – The PROBLEM Started in the Garden (https://gr8relate.com/video-courses/problem-started-in-the-garden/)
- 05D – The PROBLEM Creates and Bleak Future for Relationships (https://gr8relate.com/video-courses/problem-creates-a-bleak-future-for-relationships/)
- 12B – Creating the Relationship You Want (https://gr8relate.com/video-courses/creating-the-relationship-you-want/)

TWO CIRCLES

1. _____ / _____
2. _____
3. _____

1. _____ / _____
2. _____
3. _____

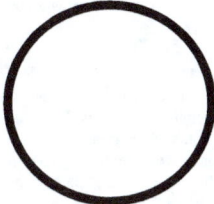

The PROBLEM and 4 Mistakes

The PROBLEM – Make Everything about ME

- Take everything personally by making your "ME" flash
- Live only by appetites, impulses, and pleasures
- Don't think— react/respond to everything emotionally
- Be happy, satisfied, and content only if people and circumstances are treating you right
- Only consider others when there is something in it for YOU.

> **James 3:16 –** Where envy and self-seeking exist, confusion and every evil thing are there.
> **Philippians 2:3 –** Let nothing be done through selfish ambition or conceit, but in lowliness of mind let each esteem others better than himself.

Operate on Opinion and Emotions – **The POLITICIAN**

- When we can't find or don't know the facts – we tend to "fill in the blanks"
- Opinion = judgment or belief not founded on certainty or proof; seem to be true or probable
- Emotions are RESPONDERS and often UNTRUSTWORTHY
- Objectivity = How it IS
- Subjectivity = How it FEELS
- "Who is my "who-said-so"?

> **Judges 21:25 –** In those days there was no king in Israel; everyone did what was right in his own eyes.
> **Proverbs 3:5-6 –** Trust in the LORD with all your heart, and lean not on your own understanding; in all your ways acknowledge Him, and He shall direct your paths

Keep the Past in the Present – **The VICTIM**

- Do not understand the power of forgiveness
- Do not understand the power of confession
- Do not understand that the PAST IS OVER
- Do not understand you are being controlled
- Good relationships leave a trail of resolved issues

> **Luke 17:3 –** And if he sins against you seven times in a day, and seven times in a day returns to you, saying, 'I repent,' you shall forgive him.
> **1 John 1:9 –** If we confess our sins, He is faithful and just to forgive us our sins and to cleanse us from all unrighteousness.

Wear a Mask – **The ACTOR**

- Acting or pretending, not being a REAL person
- "Walking on eggshells," dance around problems
- Not willing to seek or share the truth
- IMPLIES – I'm free to lie, but not free to tell the truth
- It takes 2 REAL people to have a REAL relationship

> **Ephesians 4:15 –** …but, speaking the truth in love, may grow up in all things into Him who is the head— Christ

Try to Change Others – **The DICTATOR**

- You think others should never be free to choose their path because they will mess things up
- You believe that other people must change to be like you want them
- You assign them a "JOB" to make you happy
- Reality is that the heart of a relationship is to know others for who they are and still accept, value, and love them.

> **Galatians 5:1 –** Stand fast therefore in the liberty by which Christ has made us free, and do not be entangled again with a yoke of bondage.
> **Galatians 5:13 –** For you, brethren, have been called to liberty; only do not use liberty as an opportunity for the flesh, but through love serve one another.

242 Spring Park Drive, Ste A   Midland, Texas 79705   Phone: 432-682-6823   https://gr8relate.com   Email: heben@gr8grp.com

Personal Plan Form

1. THERE—Goals, Desired Outcomes (Picturable, Measurable, Specific)	Date	

Benefits for me:	**Supports my values of:**

2. HERE—Current Reality	•
•	•
•	•
•	•
•	•
•	•
•	•
•	•

3. PATH—Actions	**Progress Measures**	**Partners**	**Date**
	Date Prepared		

This form is available as a Microsoft Word document for completion on a computer

Learn From The Past to Plan For The Future

Question 1: What were your greatest accomplishments in the last 12 months? Even if the last 12 months were the worst of your life, odds are, if you look hard enough, there's something somewhere to be proud of. If it was great, that makes answering the question even easier. After you've listed all your accomplishments, think about each one in detail. Identify several takeaways for each - what you learned or were reminded of by it.

Question 2: What were your biggest disappointments in the last 12 months? Practically every company and individual resists analyzing their mistakes. That's a shame because this is where great learning can happen. No matter how well everything is going, everyone makes mistakes. The trick here is to examine what preceded them, what you could have done differently, and how you can prevent making the same mistakes in the future. Even though the last 12 months were great, you will likely have some disappointments, both personally and professionally. As you did with your accomplishments, list your biggest disappointments - and then identify several takeaways for each one.

Question 3: How did you limit yourself in the past 12 months, and how can you remove those limits in the next 12 months? Were there certain actions you took or didn't take that came back to haunt you? Bring these actions to the surface, shine a light on them, and, most importantly, determine what you want to do differently now and in the future. Once again, make a list and identify the takeaways. For example, when I don't review my goals daily, I react and respond, getting pulled into what's currently happening and distracted from what may be more important. That reduces my actions on my goals. The takeaway: Commit to using the Daily Focus Form, and schedule key actions on my current day calendar to remind me.

Question 4: What did you learn from your answers to the first three questions? This is where you can get the best benefit from this exercise. Remember, the purpose of the exercise is not simply to know you and your business better, but actually use what you learn to help the next 12 months. What are your main takeaways from the first three questions? What do you now know about yourself or your business that you didn't realize or weren't thinking about before? Here are two items from my list...

- Creating products, coaching, and teaching are my biggest accomplishments. Therefore, it's easy to spend time daily creating materials and clarifying how to improve the material.
- A limiting factor is not focusing on attracting and acquiring more people to the material that I love to create. Marketing is inadequate, often ignored, and difficult for me.

Get as many takeaways as possible, because that is how you put your learning into reality. These takeaways can help make the next 12 months great. Of course, it's not enough to just make your list (although that, by itself, will get you part way there). You still need to take this information and USE IT! And that's where our final question comes in...

Question 5: How can you use this information to make the next 12 months great? The idea is to take everything that surfaced in your answers to the first 4 questions and build it into your schedule, your interactions, your management style, and so on. This may alter your goals or help you achieve them. Whatever you do, make sure you create goals first. For example, after I created my goals, I also added some specific actions to help me accomplish them.

- Started each morning with my Daily Focus Form.
- Block out marketing time on my weekly calendar
- Connect to some good marketing resources

S.M.A.R.T. Goals

S—SPECIFIC: The devil is in the specific details

- Clear, specific, and picturable
- Exactly what you want in concrete terms
- You will know your objective is specific enough if:
    - everyone involved knows the specifics of their involvement
    - everyone involved understands and is clear about the desired end result
    - your objective is free from jargon
    - you've defined all your terms
    - you've used only appropriate language
- These are not clear objectives
    - Increase quality time with my wife
    - Improve my writing skills
    - Create a more positive home environment
    - Regularly follow up with team members and direct reports
- These are good objectives
    - Spend at least 15 minutes each weekday morning with my wife
    - My small group rates my next three articles at 3.5 or better (1 to 5 scale)
    - Spend 30 to 60 minutes with each child each week
    - Meet for 15 minutes each workday morning to discuss yesterday's and today's top 3 tasks

S	• Specific: clear, picturable, free of jargon
M	• Measurable: you and others can know it was done (quantity, dollars, time, quality...)
A	• Acceptable ; within your control / influence, practical, realistic
R	• Result-Oriented: serves the organization's purpose and objectives, results not actions
T	• Time-bound: clear target date, deadline for completion

M—MEASURABLE: Critical Element

- You will know you've achieved your objective because the metric is the evidence. Others can know too! It becomes your statement of success.
- Objectives must have some method of tracking progress, measuring success over time
- Current Reality (HERE) is imperative for metrics
    - How would you measure weight loss if you did not know how much you weighed?
    - How do you measure employee retention if you do not know the current turnover?
    - Establish baselines (current reality) and measure progress from that point
- Objectives are not masters; they are servants supporting personal / company values and purpose
- Define the deliverables, documents, products, and accomplishments desired

HERE (Current Reality) Checklist

Did you use your Future Result as a reference point in describing current reality?

End Result	Current Reality
100% on-time delivery	89% on-time delivery in last 3 months
$48 million in annual sales	$31 million in sales in past fiscal year

Have you described the relevant picture? It must be relevant to the Future Result. No unrelated details.

End Result	Irrelevant Details
100% on-time delivery	Product packaged in blue box
$48 million in annual sales	Sales tax is captured at point of sale

Have you included the whole picture? It is not enough to say "I don't have (my future result)".

Rather Than	Write
We don't have a quality program	We don't have a formal system although people see a need for more quality in our products. Customer surveys report dissatisfaction with our current quality. We have a training specialist in-house that has had some experience with quality, and the management team is overworked and a bit resistant to any change right now.

Translate assumptions and editorials into objective news reports. We just want facts. Objective current reality allows the design of effective actions to help create the results we want.

Editorial	Facts
We don't have any business trying to go after business outside our niche market	We have tried to do business outside of our market, but we got only a small return on our investment. We didn't know how to do it.

Have you told the story without exaggeration? Better or worse than reality is not helpful.

Exaggeration	Current Reality
Our products are rated the best	One of three product surveys rated us #1. The other two rated us #4.
We have the worst record on safety	We had 9 near misses and 1 minor accident this past year

Did you state what reality is or how it got that way? Just describe "right now", not the past.

"The Journey"	Current Reality
We bought a new kettle for the plant, and by the time we installed it, the sales guys had drummed up so many new orders that we couldn't keep up. So we had to put on a new shift, but they were untrained and we didn't make a lot of headway, but our costs went up. The customers weren't getting their orders when we promised, and everyone was mad at us and blaming us, but it was really the fault of the sales guys over promising again.	Capacity is strained, more orders than we can handle. Sales and manufacturing are not coordinated. New people have taken more time than we thought to come up to speed. Costs up from adding new shift.

Have you included all the facts you need? Leaving an element out of current reality is the same as not giving the whole story.

Current sales	Current management strategies and attitudes
Current market trends	Current job market and hiring practices
Current market share	Current systems
Current competition	Current talent of members of the organization
Current financial conditions	Current core competencies
Current product quality	Current decision-making process
Current distribution system	Current business approach
Current capacity	Available resources
What you need	What you do not know
What could help	What could hurt

242 Spring Park Drive, Ste A   Midland, Texas 79705   Phone: 432-682-6823   https://gr8relate.com   Email: info.gr8relate@gr8grp.com

Pursuing their BEST
– In Work, In Life, In Love

Daily Focus Form   Date: ___/___/___

Directions

1. Do MY PROJECTS and MY CONTACTS before you do MY TODAY
2. Schedule three 60-minute slots today for items below
3. Write and review items for 7 and 30 days for your projects
4. Write all intends or ideas on the other side of this sheet
5. 1-week rule – Delete, Do, Schedule, or list on back

Time Principles

1. Limited Resource
2. Inflexible Resource
3. Always More Things to Do Than Time Available
4. **Focus (Not Efficiency) is the Key to Mastering Time**

MY FOCUS FOR TODAY (No more than 3!)

Top 3	Next 3-5

MY CONTACTS

People I need to contact today to help me accomplish my goals and projects

Could Help My Goals / Projects	Follow Up or Waiting on Them
•	•
•	•
•	•
•	•

MY PROJECTS

3-5 things I need to do in the next 7 and 30 DAYS to move each project forward

Next 7 Days	Next 30 Days
PROJECT 1 –	
PROJECT 2 –	
PROJECT 3 –	
PROJECT 4 –	

242 Spring Park Drive, Ste A   Midland, Texas 79705   Phone: 432-682-6823   https://gr8relate.com   Email: info.gr8relate@gr8grp.com

Focus Triangle

Instructions

1. List items that you need to do in the **INTEND** section. Use the back for more.
2. Review the INTEND list and write 1 to 3 that you commit to do today in the **COMMIT** section.
3. Review the INTEND list and write up to 6 items you will ATTEMPT to do today.
4. All other items stay on your INTEND list to be reviewed tomorrow or in the near future.

COMMIT

ATTEMPT

INTEND

ENDNOTES

1   The Leader's Handbook: Making Things Happen;
    Getting Things Done, Peter R. Scholtes
2   A. R., Fausset, A. R., Brown, D., & Brown, D.
    (1997). A commentary, critical and explanatory, on
    the Old and New Testaments
3   *The Fulfilled Family: God's Design for Your Home,*
    John MacArthur, p. 16

Worship:
An Awesome
Journey
Of Faith

Worship:
An Awesome
Journey
Of Faith

Kenneth G. Symes

ARPress
45 Dan Road Suite 5
Canton MA 02021
Hotline: 1(888) 821-0229
Fax: 1(508) 545-7580

Ordering Information:

Quantity sales. Special discounts are available on quantity purchases by corporations, associations, and others. For details, contact the publisher at the address above.

Printed in the United States of America.
ISBN-13:   Softcover   979-8-89330-659-0

              eBook   979-8-89330-658-3

              Hardback   979-8-89356-199-9

Library of Congress Control Number: 2024902509

"All Bible quotations are taken from The King James Version"